The Classic
WHISKEY
HANDBOOK

The Classic
WHISKEY
HANDBOOK

AN ESSENTIAL COMPANION TO
THE WORLD'S FINEST WHISKIES

— IAN WISNIEWSKI —

LORENZ BOOKS
NEW YORK • LONDON • SYDNEY • BATH

This first edition published in 1998 by Lorenz Books
27 West 20th Street, New York, NY 10011

LORENZ BOOKS are available for bulk purchase for sales promotion and for premium use. For details, write or call the
manager of special sales: Lorenz Books, 27 West 20th Street, New York, NY 10011; (800) 354-9657

Lorenz Books is an imprint of
Anness Publishing Limited

ISBN 1 85967 660 X

Publisher: Joanna Lorenz
Project Editor: Zoe Antoniou
Designer: Nigel Partridge
Cocktail Recipes: Oona van den Berg, Norma Miller and Stuart Walton
Stylists: Clare Louise Hunt and Judy Williams
Photographers: Steve Baxter, David Jordan and William Lingwood
Jacket photographer: William Lingwood

Printed and bound in Singapore

Three sets of equivalent measures have been provided in the cocktail recipes, as bar measures, metric and imperial. It is
essential that units of measurement are not mixed within each recipe. 1 measure=⅛ of a gil=22.5ml.

1 3 5 7 9 10 8 6 4 2

Contents

INTRODUCTION

Although whisky has long been established as an international speciality, it is in fact a perfect example of something that began as a practicality. Initially, whisky was distilled by monks and farmers as a means of using up surplus grain, and it was taken as a medicinal drink. It subsequently developed into an ultimate luxury as the art of distilling became an ever-more specialized craft.

Far more than just a social icon, whisky has played an important role in the history and culture of various peoples and countries, ensuring that whisky has a great story to tell. This applies particularly to the Scots and the Irish, who were the first to distil whisky, and who took this knowledge with them when they emigrated to North America, thus establishing the whisky tradition in both the USA and Canada.

Whisky is essentially produced from grain and water, using the same distillation process as other grain-based spirits such as vodka and gin. But what distinguishes whisky from these other spirits is the ageing process, and the years of maturation in oak barrels that yields an incredible range and depth of character and flavour. Whether it is served neat or mixed, as an aperitif, cocktail or digestif, whisky really is in a class of its own.

While Scotland, Ireland, the USA and Canada have achieved the most prominent reputations for producing whisky, some other countries also distill a variety of "local" whiskies, including Japan, South Korea, New Zealand, India, Brazil and Spain. Moreover, even neighbouring distilleries in Scotland produce some entirely different whiskies, and consequently there really is a world of choice among them. This is due to many factors, such as the type of grain used, the water source and, of course, the distiller's own style.

Variety also extends to the spelling of the word "whisky". In Scotland and Canada the word is spelt "whisky", while other countries such as Ireland and the USA add an "e", spelling it "whiskey". The name developed as the practice of distillation spread across Europe, and originated from various terms such as the French *eau-de-vie,* the Scottish and Irish *uisge beatha,* or the Latin *aqua vitae,* which all translate as "the water of life".

ABOVE: A classic whisky decanter and glasses.

OPPOSITE: Rob Roy, an important figure in Scottish history, seals a promise with a drink.

THE WORLD OF WHISKY

The practice of distillation is thought to have been developed by the Arabs and Chinese, who began distilling perfume from flowers and plants around 3000BC. Irish monks may well have acquired this knowledge from the Arabs as early as the sixth century, and applied it to the fermented drinks and primitive beers produced from grain. The resulting spirit developed a reputation for curing various illnesses as well as promoting longevity.

IRELAND AND THE FIRST WHISKIES

The history of whisky probably begins in Ireland. Irish whiskey is thought to pre-date Scotch whisky and, historically, it was more popular. An early

ABOVE: An early Irish whiskey still, in a painting dated 1840.

LEFT: The Jameson Distillery was founded in Ireland in 1780.

RIGHT: A portrait of Dr Johnson, by Sir Joshua Reynolds.

devotee of Irish whiskey was Queen Elizabeth I (1533–1603), who may have been introduced to it by Sir Walter Raleigh. During a visit to his estate in Ireland, Raleigh recorded in his diary that he had received "a supreme present of a 32 gallon cask of the Earl of Cork's home distilled uisce beatha".

Irish whiskey continued to receive accolades from other eminent sources. Peter the Great of Russia (1672–1725) said that "of all wines, the Irish spirit is the best". Similarly, in his *Dictionary of the English Language* first published in 1775, Dr Johnson describes "uisce beatha. It is a compounded distilled spirit, being drawn on aromaticks; and the Irish sort is particularly distinguished for its pleasant and mild flavour." Dr Johnson had also visited the White Horse Inn in Edinburgh, after which the famous blend takes its name.

By the end of the eighteenth century there were almost 2,000 stills producing whiskey in Ireland, with

the most renowned distilleries in Dublin. This included Jameson, founded in 1780, and its long-time rival Power's, established in 1791. The Old Bushmills Distillery in County Antrim is the world's oldest distillery. It gained its licence in 1608, although its history of distilling dates from 1276.

During the nineteenth century, Irish whiskey was very popular in the USA, where hundreds of different brands could be found. However, when Prohibition was established (1919–33), the dominant status of Irish whiskey was diminished. Irish whiskey also suffered a number of other setbacks during the twentieth century. The 1916 War of Independence in Ireland, followed by civil war from 1919–21, caused havoc for whiskey distillers and during the ensuing trade war with England, Irish whiskey was excluded from Britain and the British Empire. However, it is once again enjoying international acclaim.

THE DEVELOPMENT OF SCOTCH WHISKY
The Irish monks who brought Christianity to Scotland between the ninth and thirteenth centuries may have also passed on the knowledge of distillation. However, it is also

ABOVE: The history of Scotch whisky is linked to the clans – a member of the Buchanan clan is shown here.

RIGHT: The historical evolution of the Mackinlay's bottle design.

possible that Scottish farmers were already distilling whisky from their surplus barley. The earliest historical reference to Scotch whisky dates from 1494, with an entry in the Exchequer Rolls listing "eight bools of malt to Friar John Cor wherewith to make aqua vitae". This would have been enough to make approximately 1,500 bottles, which indicates that distillation was already well established at this time. Similarly, during King James IV's visit to Inverness in September 1506, his treasurer's accounts from the 15th and 17th of the month record, "for aqua vitae to the king ..." and "for ane flacat of aqua vite to the king", which is understood to refer to a locally produced spirit.

A Scottish distillery is first mentioned in the Acts of the Scottish Parliament in 1690. This was the Ferintosh Distillery owned by Duncan Forbes of Culloden. However, an earlier reference to distilling in a private house in the parish of Banffshire dates from 1614, when a thief was charged with breaking into a private house and was reported to have upset some "aqua vitie".

Significant improvements to the distilling process during the sixteenth and seventeenth centuries were partly due to the dissolution of the monasteries in 1536. Monks, who were the leading exponents of distillation, began to share their knowledge with the outside world. As the quality of whisky improved, so did the level of consumption. The

Scottish Parliament soon saw this as an opportunity for taxation, and the first Excise Act in 1644 established the level of duty on whisky.

After the Union of the Parliaments in 1707, when Scotland came under English rule, the English tried to take control of Scotland's distilling industry. However, legislation was confused and consequently difficult to enforce, and this led to a boom in illicit distilling. Smuggling soon became a way of life for many distillers, and there was no sense of immorality attached to this illegal trade. Even some ministers of the Kirk (Scottish church) made storage space available under their pulpits, and coffins were used to smuggle whisky away from the excisemen.

By 1777, there were only eight licensed distilleries in Scotland, although in Edinburgh alone there were probably

around 400 illicit stills. In the Highlands, illegal stills were cunningly concealed, and one notorious location was in a nook under a hill, where the smoke from the peat fire could be re-routed to come out of a cottage chimney further down the road. Smugglers cooperated with each other and sent signals across the hills as a warning of any impending raids. Even though around 14,000 stills were being confiscated annually, more than half of Scotland's total whisky production remained illicit.

The only obvious solution to the illegal whisky trade was to introduce reforms that would enable licensed whisky production to become a profitable enterprise. Consequently, the Duke of Gordon (on whose estate illicit distilling took place) proposed an Act of Parliament, which was passed in 1823, and this laid the foundation for the Scotch whisky industry. A £10 annual fee was established for each distillery, together with a set payment per gallon of proof spirit. The Act had the desired effect of controlling the whisky industry, and Glenlivet became the first licensed distillery in 1824. Smuggling virtually disappeared over the following decade as numerous distilleries became licensed (some of which were established on the site of former illicit distilleries).

TOP LEFT: *An early distilling scene in Scotland.*

TOP RIGHT: *One in a series of Johnnie Walker cartoons, showing here a "cask expert testing the soundness of a cask".*

LEFT: *Highland Park Distillery; casks make a significant contribution to the eventual character of the whisky.*

The popularity of Scotch whisky continued to grow for a number of reasons. Queen Victoria's visits to Balmoral Castle (purchased by the Queen in 1848) made Scotland, and all things Scottish, highly fashionable among the English. Scotch whisky also benefitted from a temporary decline in brandy production during the late nineteenth century, which was due to the destruction of many French vineyards by *phylloxera* (a deadly insect). As stocks of French brandy dwindled, Scotch whisky began to replace them and became more established as a digestif in the process.

There were also various technological advances around this time. Until the early nineteenth century, distilleries used copper pot stills to produce malt whisky, whereas the development of the Continuous still in the 1830s led to the production of grain whisky. This style of whisky was smoother and milder than malt whisky, which outside Scotland was generally considered to be too intense. Blending both types of whisky was a new concept, pioneered in the 1860s by Andrew Usher & Co. of Edinburgh, and this technique yielded a lighter, very appealing whisky.

THE AMERICAN APPROACH

The whiskey tradition in the USA stems from the original Scottish and Irish immigrants who settled throughout Pennsylvania, Maryland and Virginia. They cultivated grains

ABOVE: The Glenlivet Distillery was the first in Scotland to gain a licence in 1824.

RIGHT: Whisky smugglers on the Scottish coast, painted in 1792.

from their homelands, such as rye, barley and wheat, and used any surplus grain to produce whiskey. They called this *usquebach* (pronounced "whiskee-bah"), which was subsequently abbreviated to "whiskey". Early settlers in Virginia and Carolina were introduced to corn (maize) by the native Americans, which was also used to make whiskey, and eventually became a principal ingredient for bourbon.

The motive for distilling whiskey may well have been entirely commercial from the beginning, as it was far more profitable to transport and sell whiskey than grain. While it was considered a useful medicinal drink, whiskey's popularity was boosted by a decline in rum production, when heavy taxations on molasses from 1733 made rum distilling prohibitively expensive. Another important development was the Corn Patch and Cabin Rights Act in 1776, under which the General Assembly of the State of Virginia offered free land to any settler who would move to Kentucky (then part of Virginia), build a house, start a farm and raise corn. About 300 Scottish and Irish families from southern

Pennsylvania took up the offer and moved west. Among the early settlers were the Samuels family, who established the Maker's Mark Distillery, and Evan Williams, a Virginian who came to Kentucky and founded Kentucky's first commercial distillery on Louisville's Main Street in 1783 (a brand of bourbon still bears his name).

Another significant arrival in Kentucky, in 1786, was a presbyterian clergyman turned baptist preacher named Elijah Craig, who also began producing whiskey in 1789. Indeed, it is Reverend Craig who is popularly attributed with having "invented"

ABOVE: James Cagney is arrested for producing alcohol during Prohibition, in the film The Roaring Twenties.

RIGHT: A bottle of Jack Daniel's Whiskey and two early bottle labels.

bourbon. According to legend, a barrel-maker who was working strips of wood into curved staves by heating them over a fire accidentally charred one of the staves, but still used it in a barrel. Possibly due to a sense of economy, Reverend Craig decided to use the barrel for his whiskey. This "mistake" yielded a whiskey that was smoother and more flavourful, and the tradition of using charred barrels for bourbon began.

The importance of ageing whiskey was also discovered by chance. As casks of bourbon were stored to wait for the spring rise of the rivers before being transported by barge, it was realized that whiskey improved with age. In addition, by the time Kentucky became the nation's fifteenth state in 1792, its whiskey makers were also combining corn with the more traditional rye, having discovered that corn yielded whiskey with a sweeter finish.

Many renowned bourbon distilleries boomed in the nineteenth century. Jack Daniel founded what is now the oldest registered distillery in the USA in 1866. According to legend, Jack Daniel began to learn the art of distillation at the age of seven in the Lincoln County area, Tennessee.

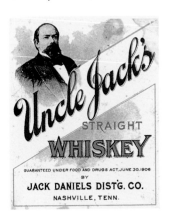

Similarly, in 1880 James Beam joined the family whiskey business that had been founded in 1795 by his grandfather Jacob Beam, and which is now known as the Jim Beam Distillery.

In 1870, a Louisville chemist called George Garvin Brown was the first to sell bourbon in sealed bottles, rather than from casks. This increased consumer confidence in a product that was commonly diluted or adulterated with inferior brands when sold from barrels. Brown went on to found his own distillery, and the Brown-Forman Corporation now has an extensive spirits portfolio.

The success of bourbon helped push back the frontier of the wild west, and by 1900 there were hundreds of distilleries in Kentucky, as well as neighbouring Indiana and Ohio. During Prohibition, some brands continued to be sold for medicinal purposes. It was not until 1964 that the USA government introduced strict regulations for bourbon production, and gave the term a legal basis.

CANADIAN AND OTHER WHISKIES

Canada's first distillery is thought to have been founded in 1668, and Canadian whisky was already well established, particularly around Quebec, by the early nineteenth century. After a temporary decline during and after the First World War, whisky production in Canada recovered when Prohibition ended in the USA, which is Canadian whiskies' main export market.

Whisky is also produced in various other countries, including Wales, Spain, Germany, Japan, New Zealand, India and Brazil. These "local" whiskies enjoy a loyal following.

TOP LEFT: A master distiller "noses" a bourbon sample.

TOP RIGHT: The Old Bushmills Distillery, the oldest whiskey distillery in the world, established in 1608.

BOTTOM: A selection of bottle labels from Canada, Japan and Wales.

BOTTLE AND LABEL DESIGNS

Whisky was first sold straight from the still or from casks. It was not until around the late nineteenth century that distillers began to bottle their whiskies, because of growing concern that they were being adulterated with inferior brands when sold from the cask. Even if there was no "foul play", selling whisky from the cask still meant that the distiller had little control over its quality or flavour, since it would continue to mature when left in the cask.

If bottling whisky was initially a practical measure, it rapidly developed into an art of its own. Distillers soon realized that a label on the bottle was an ideal way of advertising the characteristics of their brands. Also, increasingly sophisticated styles of packaging,

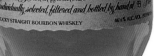

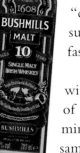

CLOCKWISE FROM TOP LEFT: The Glenfiddich Clan Series, McGibbon's Golfing Series, Alfred Dunhill Whisky, Blanton's Bourbon and two distinctive label designs (centre).

including ceramic flasks and decanters, took this art onto a different level. Some of the packaging designs capitalize on traditional associations, such as Scotland's golfing heritage, and, of course, the Scottish clans. The Glenfiddich Clan Series features presentation tins bearing eighteenth-century oil paintings of Clan Chieftains, which are reproduced from originals held in the Scottish National Gallery. Similarly, bourbon takes its cue from Kentucky's renowned thoroughbred horses, with bottles of Blanton's featuring a stopper complete with a model of a racehorse.

The exclusive "lifestyle" appeal of Scotch whisky has also led to the production of some "designer brands", launched by fashion houses such as Burberry's and Dak's, and the tobacco and fashion concern, Alfred Dunhill.

For anyone who is unfamiliar with the enormous range of whisky styles available, miniatures are a great way to sample them. Presentation packs such as the collection of The Classic Malts include six of Scotland's finest malt whiskies, one from each of Scotland's whisky-producing regions.

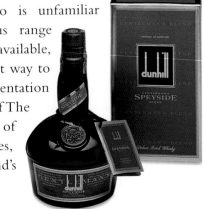

EARLY ADVERTISEMENTS

Advertising has long been an important part of the whisky trade. The style in which whisky companies have promoted their brands over the centuries provides a fascinating insight into the "social history" of whisky.

An advertising campaign would often identify its brand with a character that would appear in a series of advertisements. The Johnnie Walker figure is a prime example, having his own collection of stories which took on a life of their own. The Johnnie Walker figure also appeared in many cartoons in the British *Punch* magazine that particularly reflected the social mores of the times.

These Johnnie Walker campaigns also show how whisky has enjoyed close links with a number of sporting activities. Some early advertisements depict traditionally male pursuits, such as shooting or dog racing. Also, Scotch whisky capitalizes on Scotland being widely regarded as the home of golf, with its traditional links courses, and this has provided some evocative imagery.

Many whisky producers have used humour effectively to get their message across.

One Haig whisky campaign showed an American dandy saluting the Statue of Liberty, whose torch had been replaced by a bottle of Scotch whisky. Similarly, a Dewar's campaign, entitled "Highland Games", showed a Scotsman testing his strength with a tower of Scotch whisky cases in place of a caber, while he conquered the world in the process.

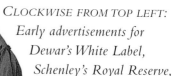

CLOCKWISE FROM TOP LEFT: Early advertisements for Dewar's White Label, Schenley's Royal Reserve, King George IV with the caption "Say when, Man!", Buchanan's Black & White, Haig Whisky and Johnnie Walker dating from 1929 (centre).

15

THE TYPES OF WHISKY

The world's most renowned whiskies, Scotch, Irish, Canadian and American, each have their own unique range of styles and characteristics. This is because various factors determine the eventual flavour of a whisky, and the following are some of the most important: the type of grain or combinations of grain that are used; the type of yeast used to affect fermentation; the local water source; the length of the maturation period; the kind of barrels that are used for storage; the climatic conditions during maturation; whether the whiskies are blended and, of course, the distiller's own style. These factors ensure that even neighbouring distilleries can produce contrasting whiskies, let alone distilleries in other regions and countries.

ABOVE: Ultima, a blend from Justerini & Brooks, is made up of 128 malt and grain whiskies.

LEFT: Single malt whiskies: Loch Dhu and Knockando.

RIGHT: A selection of blended Scotch whiskies: Chivas Regal, Passport and White Horse.

MALT WHISKIES

Malt whiskies are made using malted barley, with single malts being the product of a single distillery. Scotland and Ireland both produce malt whiskies that are prized by connoisseurs as the finest examples of the distiller's art. Aromas and flavours can range quite dramatically from one malt to another. Irish malt whiskey may have overtones of oloroso sherry, vanilla and honey in the bouquet, with a fruity sweetness and a soft, grainy finish. Scotch malt whiskies range in style according to the region in which they have been produced and matured. Elegant aromas and flavours can span fruit, nuts, and a range of spices such as cinnamon and nutmeg, balanced by a clean, light finish. At the other end of the scale, malts can incorporate peat, seaweed, malt, heather and smokiness in their aromas and flavours.

GRAIN WHISKIES

Grain whiskies are frequently produced using corn (maize) as well as malted barley. While a small number are bottled as single grain

16

whiskies, their role is principally for use in blended whisky, where they will contribute a vigour and freshness.

BLENDED WHISKIES

Malt and grain whiskies can be blended together to produce an enormous variety of styles. Irish blended whiskies yield a rich complexity that incorporates malty, nutty, fruity, lemony and spicy notes, with a soft, oaky, biscuity finish. Scotch grain whisky's mildness combines with malt whisky to yield a vast range of blended styles, which range from silky smooth, fruity, oaky elegance and sweetness with a clean, dry finish, through to a full-bodied, malty and rather smoky character.

Canadian whisky is renowned as the lightest of the world's blended whiskies. It has a mild, smooth and delicate flavour, reflecting

the combination of rye, barley and corn, and the art of blending different whiskies together. American blended whiskey is made from cereal grains, including corn, rye and winter wheat, and has a rich, deep, smooth flavour.

BOURBON

Bourbon is America's most famous whiskey. It ranges from an incredibly rich flavour with a balanced sweetness, to more elegant styles with a fruity, nutty, floral nose, rich, soft creamy flavours and a deliberately short finish. Bourbon's unique character is partly due to the ageing process, which has its own specialist approach and practices.

TOP LEFT: Irish whiskies: Bushmills Malt, Midleton Very Rare and Jameson.

TOP RIGHT: Two prominent Canadian brands: Schenley and Gibson's.

RIGHT: Two American whiskies: Gentleman Jack and Jack Daniel's.

OTHER AMERICAN WHISKIES

Tennessee whiskey is produced in a similar way to bourbon but it is also subjected to an additional "mellowing" process. The resulting whiskey is an exceptionally smooth, rich and mellow flavoured spirit, with some traces of smokiness. American rye whiskies are made with a high proportion of rye, although wheat and barley may also be added. The flavours are typically smooth and rich. A sour mash is the basis for many American whiskies, involving a process of fermentation that uses yeast from a previous mash. This produces subtle, smooth, and mellow flavoured whiskies.

THE ART OF SERVING

Whisky can be served neat or mixed, as an aperitif (before a meal), a digestif (after a meal) or as a cocktail.

APERITIFS

A traditional aperitif of blended Scotch, Canadian or American whisky is typically served neat or with ice ("on the rocks"), either in a tumbler or a goblet-shaped glass. The most favourite accompaniments are spring water, soda water, and mixers such as lemonade, ginger ale and cola. Irish whiskey is usually drunk mixed half-and-half with water, as this helps to bring out the flavour. The ideal mixer for a Scotch malt is the spring water that is also used as part of the actual whisky-making process.

DIGESTIFS

Malt whisky is an ideal digestif. It is best served in a tulip-shaped glass, as the wide waist and narrow rim channels the aroma far better than a tumbler. After pouring a measure of malt whisky, the glass should be warmed by cupping it in the hand, and swirling to release the aromas. While malt whisky is often sipped neat, the Scottish custom is to add a little still water to reveal the complexity of the nose.

Austrian glass designer Georg Riedel believes he has created the ultimate glass for single malt whisky, which was developed in conjunction with various experts. Riedel's glass is an elongated thistle shape on a truncated stem. The design incorporates a small lip designed to direct the spirit on to the tip of the tongue, where sweetness is perceived, thus emphasizing the latent creaminess of top-quality single malt.

A glass decanter is an attractive way of storing as well as serving whisky. Some deluxe brands are packaged in their own unique decanters.

COCKTAILS

Cocktails extend whisky's repertoire, and among the classic whisky-based combinations are Whisky Sour, Manhattan and Mint Julep.

CLOCKWISE FROM TOP: The Riedel glass; bourbon "on the rocks"; whisky neat; whisky soda with ice and whisky neat with ice.

How Whisky is Produced

Producing whisky is a complex process that involves various different stages, each of which have an important influence upon the whisky's final character. Some important factors include the type of grain used and how it is prepared for distillation, the water source, the type of still used, the rate of distillation, the strength at which the spirit is distilled and whether it is double or triple distilled.

soaked in tanks of spring water (known as "steeps") for two to three days. It is then spread on the floor of the malting house or in Saladin boxes and left to germinate. Germination is encouraged by directing warm air through the grain, which is regularly turned. Germination is then arrested by drying the malted barley in kilns fired by peat that has been gathered from the Scottish moors. Smoke from the peat, known as the "peat reek", imparts a distinctive aroma which remains an essential characteristic of the final spirit. However, few distilleries undertake their own malting now, and much of it is supplied by centralized maltings instead.

Scotch Malt Whisky

Scotch malt whisky is made from malted barley, water and yeast. The barley is initially malted, which means that it is

Once dried, the malt is ground and this "grist" is mixed with hot spring water in a circular vessel known as a mash tun. This converts the soluble starch within the barley into a sugary liquid known as "wort". The wort is transferred to a fermenting vat, or washback, where yeast is added and the

Top: An historical illustration showing the process of distillation.

Left: The River Spey at the heart of Speyside, Scotland.

Above right: Barley, the principal ingredient of malt whisky.

process of fermentation begins, which, over the next 48 hours, converts the sugar wort into a crude alcohol similar in aroma and taste to sour beer. This crude alcohol is known as the "wash", and it is then distilled twice in a copper pot still. The wash is distilled by being heated until it vaporizes and rises within the still, before condensing back into liquid form within the cooling plant, from where it is collected.

ABOVE: Washback containers at Glenfiddich Distillery.

The resulting spirit is transferred to a vat and diluted with spring water before being transferred into casks for maturing. Both malt and grain spirit are matured in oak casks for a minimum of three years. Distillation and maturation must take place in Scotland in order to qualify for the term "Scotch whisky".

SCOTCH GRAIN WHISKY

Scotch grain whisky is made from wheat or corn (maize), which is first cooked under steam pressure for a few hours to release starches that can be converted into fermentable sugars. The cereals can then be combined with a proportion of malted barley in the mash tun and mixed with boiling water, which converts the starch into the sugar. Yeast is

TYPES OF STILL

The traditional method of making whisky uses the copper pot still, which was established throughout Europe by the sixteenth century.

The liquid wash that has been fermented and had its sugar converted into alcohol is heated until the alcoholic vapour rises inside to the top of the still's single column before condensing in a pipe, which is immersed in cold water. The pipe leads into a special container from which the alcohol can be collected. It is a laborious process as it is only possible to make spirit in batches. Scotch and Irish malt whiskies are both distilled in copper pot stills.

Technical advances came in the 1830s, with the invention of the Coffey or Patent still. This comprises two columns, with vapour from the wash rising in the first and condensing in the second. Apart from offering a continuous process, it was also less expensive to operate than a pot still, although it was equally able to produce good quality spirit. Also known as a Continuous still, this is used to produce grain whisky.

LEFT: Copper pot stills at Alt-a-Bhain Distillery, Scotland.

added to affect fermentation and produce the wash, which then passes into the continuously operating Coffey or Patent still.

BLENDING WHISKIES

Blending malt and grain whiskies to make blended whisky accounts for the vast majority of Scotch whisky sales. Blending is undertaken by a master blender, who is also known as a "nose" for obvious reasons. The blender's highly refined sense of smell will help gauge which whiskies will best complement each other, and particularly the age at which various whiskies should be blended.

The master blender decides which type of cask is most appropriate to age malt and grain spirit, either new oak or casks that were previously used to hold sherry or bourbon. Various considerations affect the length of the ageing period, including the size of cask used (ranging from around 45 to 500 litres), the strength at which the spirit is matured (for malt whisky this is usually 63.5% alcohol by volume whereas grain whisky is usually matured at 70–85%), as well as the temperature and humidity of the warehouse. Malt whisky generally takes longer to mature than grain, and is frequently left in the cask for ten years or more.

ABOVE: Date-stamping casks at Knockando Distillery.

LEFT: Workers at the Glenturret Distillery, 1905.

THE CASKS

Various types of casks, or barrels, are used for maturation, including casks previously used to hold bourbon and sherry. As the casks are porous, air passes through the wood and helps to mellow the whisky. Similarly, the whisky extracts beneficial compounds from the oak, and retains some of the natural colour of the wood.

Charred casks release compounds into the whisky at a faster rate than new oak, while casks conditioned by previously holding bourbon or sherry also release their own distinctive flavours, which add complexity to the whisky.

A proportion of whisky is lost during the ageing process due to evaporation – this is known as the "angel's share".

BELOW: Casks at the Glenturret Distillery, Scotland.

When preparing blended whisky, the master blender may use anything from 15 to 50 malt and grain whiskies, each selected for their aroma, flavour and character. The aim is to create a harmonious blend, which is more complex but also smoother than the individual whiskies. Master blenders check samples of whisky, using their nose, in a tulip-shaped glass (which best channels the bouquet), with a little fresh water to help release the aromas.

The whiskies are blended in special vats and pumped back into casks. They are left for between six and eight months when the individual whiskies are left to harmonize. This is known as the "marriage". The blended whisky is reduced to bottling strength (minimum 40% alcohol by volume within the European Union) by diluting it with water.

Blended Scotch whisky does not always carry an age statement, although when it does, this refers to the age of the youngest whisky. A deluxe blended Scotch whisky contains a higher proportion of older whiskies.

IRISH WHISKEY

One of the major differences between Irish and Scotch whisky is that the malt for Irish whiskey is dried in a closed kiln and not over a peat fire, so it does not absorb the peat reek. While Scotch whisky is distilled twice, Irish whiskey is distilled three times in copper pot stills. Corn may also be used in a mash with malted barley to make lighter styles of Irish whiskey. After the third and final distillation, Irish whiskey is matured in oak barrels that were formerly used to hold either Irish whiskey, sherry, bourbon or even rum.

Another important difference between Irish and Scotch blended whiskies is that Scottish distillers blend malt and grain whiskies, many of which may be bought in from other distilleries, whereas in Ireland the whiskies in the blend are all produced at the distillery. An Irish saying goes, "the art is in the distilling rather than in the blending".

BOURBON

Bourbon, which takes its name from the original corn whiskey made in Bourbon County, Kentucky, can be produced anywhere in the USA, though Kentucky is the only

TOP LEFT: "Nosing" a sample of Scotch whisky.

TOP RIGHT: A blender inspects a maturing American whiskey.

LEFT: Cardhu Distillery in Knockando was established in 1872.

state allowed to put its name on the bottle label. Bourbon must be made using a mash containing a minimum of 51 per cent and a maximum of 79 per cent corn. Other grains that are used include barley malt, rye and wheat. Bourbon is produced using a Continuous still, and must be aged for a minimum of two years in new white oak casks, charred on the inside, as this caramelizes some of the natural sugars in the oak. It is from this wood that bourbon takes its colour and some flavour.

OTHER AMERICAN WHISKIES

Although very similar to bourbon, Tennessee whiskey includes an extra process that occurs after distillation and before ageing. The spirit is mellowed by filtering it through layers of maple charcoal. This charcoal is typically prepared from sugar maple trees, aged for a year and burned in carefully stacked ricks in the open air (which allows any impurities to escape). The resulting charcoal is ground and packed into the mellowing vats.

American corn whiskey is a separate category from bourbon, and must be produced from a mash containing at least 80 per cent corn, and aged in charred casks or casks previously used for ageing other spirits. American rye whiskey must use a mash containing at least 51 per cent rye, and aged in newly charred oak casks.

CANADIAN WHISKY

The regulations for producing Canadian whisky do not stipulate a minimum percentage for any type of grain used, the strength at which whisky is distilled, or the type of casks used for maturation. The main directive states that Canadian whisky must "possess the aroma, taste and character generally attributed to Canadian whisky", with a minimum of three years ageing stipulated.

There are two different approaches to blending whisky in Canada. The conventional method of "post-blending" means that various mature whiskies of different characters are blended together, whereas "pre-blending", used by Canadian Club, involves blending whiskies prior to maturation. The whiskies are aged in white oak casks previously used to hold bourbon (and so charred on the inside), some of which are also recharred to effect different degrees of "wood flavouring".

ABOVE: Burning the charcoal stacks that will be used to mellow Tennessee whiskies.

LEFT: Bottling Evan Williams at the Heaven Hill Distillery.

RIGHT: Pot stills at a Suntory-owned distillery in Japan.

SCOTCH WHISKY

Scotland produces outstanding malt, grain and blended whiskies. These separate styles of whisky provide different opportunities and challenges for the distillers.

Scotch grain whiskies have a milder flavour and aroma than malt whiskies and are less influenced by geographical factors. When they are combined with malt whiskies in a blend, grain whiskies contribute both vigour and subtlety. Malt whiskies vary significantly and are classified according to the location of the distillery in which they were produced.

There are four areas that produce malts, and each produces a whisky with distinct characteristics. Lowland malt whiskies are produced in the south of Scotland and are generally the mildest of the Scotch malts. The Highlands in the north produce malt whiskies that have a range of robust flavours and aromas. Speyside malt whiskies technically come from within the area designated as the Highlands. The region's climatic conditions produce

whiskies of an identifiable character that are renowned as the finest by connoisseurs, and nearly half of Scotland's distilleries are located here. Islay malt whiskies, from the island of Islay, are the most powerful of the malts, with a distinct peat flavour.

The history of Scotch whisky is inevitably intertwined with the culture of Scotland and various traditions demand the presence of a measure or two of whisky. On New Year's Day, for example, "first footing" is an important celebration, when tradition has it that the first person to step into your house must be a tall dark stranger carrying a piece of coal (to ward off the cold) and a measure of whisky to toast the coming new year.

ABOVE: The dramatic Suilven landscape, showing the natural resources that Scotland is famous for.

LEFT: Glen Ord, one of many fine Scotch malt whiskies.

RIGHT: William Grant, whose name graces a renowned blend of Scotch whisky.

Whisky is also closely linked to the history of the clans and their pipers. Scottish armies were traditionally led into battle by pipers playing bagpipes, to inspire the soldiers as well as to terrorize the enemy. In recognition of the piper's courage, a dram (a measure) of the finest whisky was reserved for him, a tradition still observed at many Highland gatherings.

Scottish pipers were at their most heroic when leading the Jacobite risings in 1715 and 1745. These unsuccessful attempts to restore the Stuart kings to the English throne culminated in the 1745 uprising, which was led by Bonnie Prince Charlie, grandson of the last Stuart monarch. He marched south with an army led by 100 pipers, drawn from all the Scottish clans. Their story was celebrated in the old Scottish song, "The Ballad of 100 Pipers". After initial successes, the Highlanders retreated to Scotland and were pursued by the English. It was there that the Scots endured a final defeat, in the Battle of Culloden in 1746. Seagram produces a Scotch whisky called "100 Pipers", which pays tribute to their heroism.

ABOVE: An early Dewar's whisky advertisement shows a humorous drinking scene.

LEFT: A Scottish piper.

There is also a Scottish legend which stipulates that when you taste a good Scotch whisky you can hear a piper play, and if the whisky is mild you may hear two pipers; three or four if it is smooth, and five or even six if it is mellow. But, of course, if you hear 100 pipers then it must indeed be an exceptional whisky.

ROBERT BURNS

Robert Burns (1759–96), regarded as Scotland's national poet, was also a devotee of Scotland's national drink. He was born into a farming family in Alloway, a village on the river Doon. The hardship of his early farming life, which Burns bitterly resented, not to mention bouts of unrequited love, drove him to write poetry. First published in 1786, he composed narrative poems, satirical verse and songs such as "Auld Lang Syne", using Scots dialect as well as English. His genuine interest in Scottish folk songs also resulted in numerous poems written to be sung to Scottish folk tunes. This ensured his popularity amongst the Scottish gentry, as well as literary circles. However, he remained a farmer throughout his life, which gave him a joy in simple pleasures, but also meant that he had a demanding life with few rewards. In 1788, Burns became an exciseman in an attempt to balance the financial losses of farming, and his early death is thought to have stemmed from the severity of a hard-working life during his youth.

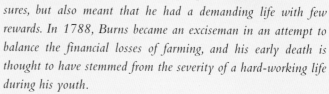

To make a Bobby Burns cocktail, stir together 20ml/4 tsp each of Scotch whisky, dry vermouth, red vermouth and a dash of Benedictine. Add ice and a maraschino cherry.

SCOTTISH DISTILLERIES

Numerous distilleries, many of which comprise historic buildings set amidst spectacular scenery, can be visited throughout Scotland. For malt whisky lovers, the ultimate journey is the Malt Whisky Trail that follows the river Spey, among the foothills of the Grampians in the region known as Speyside. The climate and geology of Speyside are ideal for producing malt whisky, so it is not surprising that almost half of Scotland's distilleries are in this area. Some distilleries are open to the public and contain visitor centres and shops.

Included on the Trail is Cardhu Distillery in Knockando, which is the only malt distillery to have been pioneered by a woman. Whisky is matured here for at least twelve years in oak casks. The Glenfiddich Distillery, Dufftown, dates from

1887 and is home to the famous malt whisky of the same name, which is the only Highland malt whisky to be bottled at the distillery.

Dating from 1786, Strathisla in Keith is the oldest working distillery in the Highlands, and produces the malt which is at the heart of Chivas Regal.

The Glenlivet was the first distillery to take out a licence, in 1824, and is home to the eponymous 12-year-old malt. Dallas Dhu Distillery in Forres, is also on the Trail. It was the last distillery to be built in the nineteenth century.

While many distilleries on the Trail are renowned for their period architecture, the Glen Grant Distillery in Speyside also has a beautiful garden that is open to visitors. It was founded in 1840 by two brothers, James and John Grant. In 1886, their descendant, Major James Grant, decided to create a woodland garden in the sheltered valley behind the distillery. It was designed to have great natural beauty, reflecting the charm and rugged grandeur of the Scottish Highlands.

Major Grant soon established the custom of inviting guests to take a stroll through the orchards past the lily pond, and up to the waterfall where the Glen Grant (or back burn, as it is

ABOVE: An early bottle label from the Glenlivet Distillery.

LEFT: The Glenlivet Distillery, Dufftown.

RIGHT: A bottle label for Dallas Dhu.

locally known) flows through a ravine. On a neighbouring foot-bridge they would enjoy a refreshing dram (a measure) of Glen Grant from a special whisky safe, situated in the rock face above the burn, and water would be drawn from the back burn to dilute their drams.

LEFT: The Cardhu Distillery.

BELOW LEFT AND ABOVE RIGHT: The Glen Grant Distillery and the bottle bearing its name.

SCOTCH WHISKY LIQUEURS

Drambuie is Scotland's most widely known liqueur. It is a mixture of malt and grain whiskies with delicious flavourings of heather honey and herbs. Its name originates from the Gaelic "an dram buidheach", which means "the drink that satisfies".

Glayva is also a favourite, and it is flavoured in a similar way to Drambuie, although it has a quantity of orange peel that makes its taste noticeably fruitier. Glayva is used in the cocktail Saracen, and is associated with the noble Scot Master Borthwick, who carried Robert the Bruce's heart back to Scotland. In an act of retaliation, he also carried the head of a Saracen, the group who had killed Robert the Bruce in battle.

MALT WHISKY DIRECTORY

The following guide explains the principal characteristics of a selection of malt whiskies that are produced in Scotland.

ABERLOUR 10 YEAR OLD

Located in the heart of Speyside, the renowned Aberlour Glenlivet Distillery dates from 1879, with the name translating from Gaelic as "mouth of the chattering burn". This is a harmonious malt, featuring subtle aromas of nutmeg

and cinnamon, together with hints of autumn fruits on the palate.

BENRIACH 10 YEAR OLD

Benriach is one of the few distilleries that still dries its own malt over a traditional peat fire on the premises. This whisky has a medium-bodied flavour, yet is rich and complex with currants and Highland peat, while the aftertaste is more dry and refined.

BENROMACH 12 YEAR OLD

This Speyside malt has recently been revived, having last been bottled as a single malt in the early 1900s. It is fruity on the nose with chocolate and toffee hints, light-bodied on the palate with fruit and spice recalling dried fruit and cinnamon, and has a clean, light finish.

BOWMORE LEGEND

This whisky comes from the Inner Hebridean island of Islay, where the distillery was established in 1779 on the shores of Loch Indaal. The malt is peaty with a touch of seaweed and geranium on the nose, while the palate has smoky hints and seaweed with a lemonade sweetness in the finish.

BOWMORE 12 YEAR OLD

This features lemon and sea salt on the nose, followed by hints of dark chocolate and pears on the palate and a good, smoky sea taste with a touch of heather honey which lingers nicely.

BUNNAHABHAIN 12 YEAR OLD

Pronounced "bu-na-ha-venn", which in Gaelic means "mouth of the river", this Islay malt is light and fresh on the nose,

and is light-to-medium-bodied with exceptional smoothness, a hint of Islay peat and a good fruity, refreshing finish.

CAOL ILA 15 YEAR OLD

This Islay malt has a deep peaty nose and is exceptionally oily on the palate, clinging to the roof of the mouth with a peaty and dark chocolate oakiness. A full-bodied whisky, it also manages to retain great subtlety and control.

CARDHU

This comes from the only malt whisky distillery that was pioneered by a woman, Elizabeth Cumming, who took over the distillery in 1872. It has an exceptionally smooth, silky and mellow taste.

CRAGGANMORE 12 YEAR OLD

Cragganmore Distillery was founded in 1869, and was built using greenstone quarried from the Craggan Mor hill. It was the first distillery to use steam locomotives in order to transport its whisky. This malt has a firm body, a malty, smoky finish, and an after-dinner style.

DALWHINNIE 15 YEAR OLD

Dalwhinnie is a Gaelic word meaning "the meeting place", which is apt for a distillery located high on the wild, windswept moors of the Grampian mountains in the northern Highlands, where it was established in 1898. At 1,000 feet above sea level, its altitude is higher than any other distillery. The whisky has a sweet, fruity aroma, and is light on the palate with a certain heathery, delicate finish.

THE EDRADOUR 10 YEAR OLD

The Edradour Distillery is highly specialized and is the smallest in Scotland,

with a weekly output rarely exceeding 600 gallons. The malt is slightly sweet on the nose, rich and smooth on the palate.

GLENFIDDICH

Glenfiddich means "valley of the deer" in Gaelic, which refers to the site near Dufftown where the distillery can be found. This is one of the world's most celebrated brands, and it is notable for its light, shimmering gold colour and purity of taste.

GLENFIDDICH EXCELLENCE 18 YEAR OLD

This is a rich, smooth whisky matured in oloroso sherry casks. The resulting sweetness is perfectly balanced by the oakiness and long lingering finish from the traditional oak casks.

GLEN GRANT

Distilled since 1840, this Speyside malt yields a clean, slightly dry first taste which opens up into a distinctive, mild, fruity finish.

GLENKINCHIE 10 YEAR OLD

The Glenkinchie Distillery was founded in 1837 and produces one of the smokiest of the Lowland malts, which has a light, delicate nose. It is particularly light and smooth, with a slightly dry finish.

THE GLENLIVET

Founded in 1824, the Glenlivet Distillery produces this well-known malt. The nose is lavish and flowery, while the palate is subtle and slightly smoky with a delicate, rounded taste.

GLENMORANGIE

The Glenmorangie Distillery was among the earliest to be licensed, in 1843, during the time when illicit distilling had been thriving in the area. Matured in wild mountain oak bourbon casks for a minimum of 10 years, this whisky has a smooth, rounded taste with a subtly perfumed bouquet.

GLEN ORD 12 YEAR OLD

This comes from the only distillery on the Black Isle Peninsula, north of Inverness, which was established in 1838. The production process is unusual in using water from two sources, lakes fed by rainfall as well as springs coming up from the water table, locally referred to as coming from "heaven and earth". Using sherry oak casks helps give the malt a smooth and rich, malty taste.

GLENROTHES

The Glenrothes Distillery, in the heart of Speyside, was established in 1879. It offers a selection of vintage malts, including the 1979 which has a full, silky-smooth flavour spanning liquorice and spice, touches of dried fruit and peat, with a spicy, dry finish.

HIGHLAND PARK 12 YEAR OLD

This is produced on the island of Orkney in the world's most northerly Scotch whisky distillery, founded in 1798. It has a rounded, smoky sweetness, which is malty and smooth with a heathery finish.

KNOCKANDO

The name is derived from the Gaelic "cnock-an-dhu", meaning "little black hill". This is a classic Speyside whisky with complexity, delicacy and fruitiness.

LAGAVULIN 16 YEAR OLD

The distillery was founded in 1816 on the Hebridean island of Lagavulin. This is a complex whisky that has considerable depth, with a smoky, peaty taste and silky dryness.

LAPHROAIG 10 YEAR OLD

The name in Gaelic means "beautiful hollow by the broad bay" and is pronounced "la-froyg". It is the only whisky to be awarded the Royal warrant

by HRH The Prince of Wales. The distillery was founded in 1815 on Islay, one of the Inner Hebrides islands. Matured in Kentucky bourbon oak casks, this malt has a distinctive flavour of peat, smoke and seaweed. It is also available in cask strength bottling at 57.3% alcohol by volume, which provides a depth of peaty taste and texture.

LOCH DHU 10 YEAR OLD

Produced at the foot of the Maanochmore "Black Hills" in the northern Highlands, this "black" whisky's darkness is achieved by using specially selected oak casks that are subjected to a process of "sweet" double

charring. This is then followed by an extended maturation period. The resulting velvety black whisky has an aroma of mint toffee. Its taste is exceptionally smooth and it has a light textured body, with warming spicy flavours and lingering notes of wild herbs.

LONGMORN 15 YEAR OLD

The Longmorn Distillery was founded in 1894 by John Duff. This malt whisky offers both elegance and a fragrant bouquet, and is also full-bodied, with a lingering, slightly sweet aftertaste. In 1994, this particularly prized single malt whisky was awarded the prestigious Gold Medal at the International Wine and Spirits Awards in London.

THE MACALLAN 10 YEAR OLD

This is a Speyside whisky with hints of almonds, pears, heather and sherry. It is very smooth on the palate, with a touch of sherry and wood. It is slightly sweet and has a well-rounded flavour.

THE MACALLAN 18 YEAR OLD

On the nose, this malt has a honeyed, wine-like sweetness, a hint of almonds, pears and heather, with a more assertive sherry character and a long, oak-flavoured, dry finish and an excellent malt flavour.

THE MACALLAN 25 YEAR OLD

This malt has heather and honey notes together with a distinctly sweet and heady nose. It is rich and full on the palate, as well as being elegant and full-bodied. The lingering finish is exceptionally smooth, while also retaining a wonderfully silky complexity.

MORTLACH 16 YEAR OLD

This Speyside whisky is complex and elegant, with sherry, smoky, peaty tones. It makes an ideal digestif.

OBAN 14 YEAR OLD

Oban is a port on the west Highland coast which dates back to the pre-historic times of Obanian stone-age culture. The distillery was one of the earliest to be

founded, in 1794, pre-dating the surrounding town. This single malt has a well-structured character, with a fresh delicate hint of peat in the aroma, which is followed by a long, smooth finish.

POIT DHUBH FINE GAELIC MALT WHISKY

Pronounced "potch ghoo", which means "black pot", this 12-year-old malt is partly matured in sherry casks, with a robust flavour and a trace of peatiness.

THE SINGLETON OF AUCHROISK

Pure, soft water is one element of this exceptionally mellow malt, with a smooth taste and rich, deep colour, which is aided by oak ageing as well as maturation in sherry casks.

TALISKER 10 YEAR OLD

Talisker is the only distillery that can be found on the Isle of Skye, which is famous for its beautiful and dramatic landscapes, as celebrated by the artist J.M.W. Turner in a painting of Loch Coruisk. This malt is a well-balanced whisky with a slightly sweet aroma that is fully flavoured. It also has a distinctive peaty taste that explodes and lingers on the palate. It is ideal for devotees of malt with a "marine" character.

BLENDED SCOTCH WHISKY DIRECTORY

BALLANTINE'S FINEST

The soft, deep, elegant aromas of this blend feature heather and honey, and suggestions of spice. On the palate it is round, deep and well-balanced with rich milk chocolate notes, together with red apple and vanilla, which linger gently.

BELL'S EXTRA SPECIAL 8 YEAR OLD

The majority of the 35 malt and grain whiskies in the blend are from United Distiller's own distilleries, and this includes Oban, Caol Ila, Dufftown and Glenkinchie, which provide complexity, texture and depth of flavour.

BLACK & WHITE

This is built around three of the key malt whiskies, Dalwhinnie, Clynelish and Glendullan, within a blend that comprises 35 malt and grain whiskies. It has an ultra smooth, mild flavour.

BURBERRY'S 12 YEAR OLD

This blend was created for Thomas Burberry (1835–1926), who was the founder of the well-known Burberry's

fashion house. Originally, Thomas Burberry gave presents of this blend to his hosts when staying at sporting estates in the Scottish Highlands. It is a full-bodied, rich, sweet and floral blend with a hint of peat. The 15 year old is a full-bodied, smooth malt with a hint of spice, oak and a smoky finish.

CHIVAS REGAL 12 YEAR OLD

The Chivas story began with a single shop established in Aberdeen in 1801. By 1843 the business had already received its first royal warrant from Queen Victoria. In 1891 the Chivas brothers created the Chivas Regal blend, and a royal warrant followed from King George V in 1923. At the heart of the blend is Strathisla malt whisky, which is delicate and mellow with a sustained finish. Among more than 30 other malts in the blend are the Glenlivet, Longmorn and Glen Grant. The result is a light smokiness with malt and a subtle hint of sweetness.

CHIVAS REGAL SPECIAL RESERVE 15 YEAR OLD

This is a sophisticated and limited edition blend that is rich, deep and complex, with delicate fruit enhanced by a soft sweetness that imparts a lingering finish.

CLAN CAMPBELL

This is named after the Campbell family, whose history dates from 1266. They rose to become one of the greatest of all the ancient clans, playing a major role in the events that shaped Scottish history. The nose of this blend is predominantly fruity, with a hint of smokiness on the medium-bodied palate, and it has a clean and light refreshing finish.

CUTTY SARK

Named after the historic clipper, "The Cutty Sark", moored at Greenwich in London, this whisky is aged for a minimum of four years and offers a delicate, flowery aroma, and is soft and clean on the palate.

DAK'S

This is a "designer" whisky available in three styles. The 12 year old has a smooth, round flavour. The 17 year old is rich on the nose and palate, providing a sustained aftertaste. The 25 year old is mature, extremely rich and smooth with a long-lasting flavour.

DEWAR'S WHITE LABEL

This is well-balanced with a medium-to-full body. A hint of smokiness in the aroma is followed by a malty sweetness and a delicately balanced smoky flavour, with a clean, dry finish.

DIMPLE 15 YEAR OLD

The Haig family began distilling in 1627, though the family established its first commercial distillery in 1824. The Dimple blend was devised in the 1890s, and its success was such that Haig received a Royal warrant from Edward VII in 1908. It has a smooth, aromatic and smoky, peaty flavour.

ALFRED DUNHILL GENTLEMAN'S SPEYSIDE BLEND

This contains around 85 per cent Speyside malts, which yield a rounded, fruity aroma and hint of peatiness that is derived from Islay malts, with a rich, fruity taste, supreme mellowness and a lingering aftertaste.

ALFRED DUNHILL OLD MASTER FINEST

This distinguished blend is composed of more than 30 aged malt and grain whiskies, some of which are more than 20 years old. The result is a balanced and fruity nose that has rich and fruity flavours, with a remarkable mellowness and sustained aftertaste.

WILLIAM GRANT'S FAMILY RESERVE

This is another well-known whisky produced by the makers of the renowned Glenfiddich malt. William Grant produced the first spirit here on Christmas Day in 1887. Containing fine malt and grain whiskies, this blend has a fine aroma with a smooth, mellow flavour.

THE FAMOUS GROUSE

The word "famous" was added to the name due to its popularity. It is smooth, medium-peated, and well-rounded, with a touch of dryness that allows the complexity of the blend to come through.

THE FAMOUS GROUSE GOLD RESERVE

This 12-year-old deluxe blend has a rich, full aroma including well-balanced oak with a hint of peach, and rich, silky fruit and oak with a clean, dry finish on the palate.

J&B RARE

This is ultra smooth and perfectly balanced, using the finest of Speyside malts, with a delicate but fragrant aroma and flavour.

J&B RESERVE 15 YEAR OLD

This blend's high malt content is balanced by grain whiskies, yielding a smooth, fragrant and delicate flavour.

JOHNNIE WALKER RED LABEL

This contains around 35 malt and grain whiskies. Its fresh aromas include

hints of vanilla and a powerful smoky malt that repeats on the palate together with spicy notes. It is full-bodied with a distinctive burst of warmth.

JOHNNIE WALKER BLACK LABEL

This is the world's leading 12-year-old deluxe blend, composed of more than 40 malt and grain whiskies that are specially selected to yield a depth and complexity of flavour. It has a full-bodied rich, smooth taste with a depth of flavour that lingers on the palate, reflecting a high proportion of powerful malts from the island of Islay.

PASSPORT

This was introduced in 1965 as a blend for the modern palate, in a distinctive green glass bottle. It contains a high proportion of Highland malts combined with lighter, sweeter Lowland whiskies to create an elegant, medium-bodied, well-balanced blend.

ROYAL SALUTE 21 YEAR OLD

Created in 1953 to commemorate the coronation of Queen Elizabeth II, this is selected from rare whiskies and is rich in malts, providing character and subtlety. Single malts within the blend include the elegant and subtle Glenlivet, the rich and mellow Strathisla, the light, dry fruitiness of Glen Grant, and Longmorn with its smooth sherried lingering aftertaste. The result is a full-bodied, balanced blend with a smooth and slightly sweet, lingering aftertaste. It is available in three presentations, Royal Blue, Royal Red and Royal Green ceramic flasks.

SEAGRAM'S 100 PIPERS

This blend is rich in Speyside malts, yielding a medium-bodied blend with a slightly sweet aftertaste.

TÉ BHEAG

The name is pronounced "chey vek", meaning "little lady", as well as a "wee dram" in colloquial Gaelic. Smooth and slightly peated, this blend has a high malt content including some rich old whiskies, with a hint of sherry from the casks in which they have been matured.

TEACHER'S HIGHLAND CREAM

With one of the highest percentages of malts among blended whiskies, this has depth, power and real character. The original William Teacher was successful during the mid-nineteenth century, and specialized in bulk blends of whisky. Highland Cream is one of Teacher's most successful blends.

VAT 69

The original recipe was developed in 1882 by William Sanderson,

founder of the House of Sanderson, one of the great Scotch whisky houses. When experimenting with over 100 whiskies, Sanderson's group of friends and experts chose the blend from vat

number 69 as the most palatable, which resulted in the brand's name. The distinctive green glass bottles display the royal warrant to supply Scotch whisky granted by Queen Elizabeth II. The blend is based on the malt of the Aultmore Distillery, in Grampian, a whisky highly regarded for its distinctive fruity flavour. The casks used for ageing whiskies that go into this blend give the whisky its sweet, rounded flavour.

WHITE HORSE

In 1801, the Lagavulin Distillery was established on the Island of Islay, initially a site of illegal distilling. This particular blend was named after the famous White Horse Tavern, which is located in Edinburgh's fashionable Canongate district. A white horse was also a symbolic object, which represented freedom and independence. Created in 1890, the blend contains more than 35 malt whiskies, including Lagavulin's smoky, peaty, Islay character and Glen Elgin and Craigellachie's soft and sweet aromatic finish.

IRISH WHISKEY

Traditionally, whiskey from Dublin was the most highly prized in Ireland, and many distilleries were founded in the city during the eighteenth century, when Dublin was one of the most important cities of the British Empire. One of the most celebrated figures in the history of Irish whiskey is John Jameson, who established his distillery in Dublin in 1780 with the eponymous brand.

While this brand triumphed in export markets, its long-time rival Power's Gold Label captured the home market. James Power established his distillery in Dublin in 1791, and was succeeded by his son in 1817, who became Sir John Power, the High Sheriff of Dublin. In 1886, Power's was one of the first brands to introduce distillery bottling. By 1891, the centenary of the distillery, the Power's brand was widely exported. Two years later, it was even exhibited at the World Fair in Chicago in the form of an enormous model of an Irish round tower, which was made with thousands of bottles of Power's Whiskey.

One of the more colourful characters in the Irish whiskey trade was Paddy Flaherty, a salesman for Cork Distilleries Company in the Munster area during the 1920–30s. He had the difficult task of building up the Cork Distilleries Company Old Irish whiskey in a market that was dominated by the Power's brand. Paddy's sales trips meant touring the pubs of various towns on his bicycle, and his arrival generated a great amount of excitement because he was known to be generous and frequently bought drinks for everyone in the pub.

ABOVE: A view of the lush, green landscape of Ireland.

LEFT: An early etching of Midleton Distillery, home of Midleton whiskey.

RIGHT: A label for Paddy whiskey.

ABOVE: An interior of an Irish pub, where the Jameson brand has a strong presence.

As Paddy's whiskey became more popular, publicans frequently ran low on stocks before Paddy came around again for the next order, so they began to contact the distillery directly. Having to ask for the "Cork Distilleries Company Old Irish whiskey" was obviously quite a mouthful, so instead the publicans simply asked for "Paddy Flaherty's whiskey". The name began to stick, and the distillery realized that this could be turned into an advantage, so Paddy Flaherty's name was added to the bottle label, and subsequently the brand name was changed to Paddy.

Ireland's two principal distilleries are now the Old Bushmills Distillery in County Antrim, which is also the oldest distillery in the world, founded in 1608, and the Old Midleton in County Cork. Both of these distilleries can be visited to view exhibits and to enjoy a whiskey tasting. The Old Jameson Distillery and museum in Bow Street, Dublin, are also open to visitors.

JAMESON'S IRISH WHISKEY

John Jameson, who is one of the most distinguished figures in the history of Irish whiskey, founded his distillery in Bow Street, Dublin, in 1780. Dublin whiskies were considered the finest in the country, and Jameson's were among the best in Dublin. Indeed, his whiskies were soon established internationally for their superior quality. Six generations later, descendants of Jameson are still producing superlative whiskies with Jameson 1780, a 12-year-old whiskey that is a fine and fitting tribute to its namesake.

CLOCKWISE FROM TOP: A painting of John Jameson, a bottle bearing his name, and an early scene showing casks about to be transported at The Old Jameson Distillery.

IRISH PUBS

Public houses have always been a very important land-mark in Ireland and traditionally they also incorporated a grocer's and post office. They continue to be popular meeting places for the Irish to indulge in good conversation, which often leads to singing. Changing pub designs led to the creation of the "snug", a small room that was perfect for more intimate social gatherings.

Needless to say, the local brands have always been the most popular whiskies to be ordered in pubs. The traditional way to serve whiskey in Ireland is with water, as this is thought to bring out its flavour. Each person adds water according to personal taste, mindful of the old Irish saying "you must never steal another man's wife, and never water another man's whiskey". However, whiskey can also be drunk neat, on the rocks or with soda water.

An Irish pub is also the best place to enjoy the *craic*, (pronounced "crack"), which is an Irish term referring to the good time that happens spontaneously when people get together, and of course Irish whiskey is a great contributor to the creation of the *craic*.

A Hot Irish is particularly popular in pubs in the winter. This can be made by studding a half lemon slice with four cloves, which is then placed in a warmed glass with a measure of Irish whiskey and a little brown sugar. Boiling water is then added, with a pinch of cinnamon to make an even more spicy flavour.

OPPOSITE, ABOVE AND BELOW: A selection of Irish pubs.

IRISH WHISKEY LIQUEURS

It is hardly surprising that the world has developed a passion for Irish cream liqueurs – they are after all a wonderful way to enjoy Irish whiskey. Indeed, since their launch in the mid-1970s, Irish cream liqueurs have been an outstanding success.
Baileys is now the world's leading liqueur brand, and it requires an awful lot of cream. In fact, Baileys accounts for an astonishing 33 per cent of Ireland's total liquid milk production, with the milk subsequently separated into double cream, before being mixed with Irish whiskey and spirits. Serve it straight up or with ice.

IRISH WHISKEY DIRECTORY

The following guide explains the characteristics of a selection of whiskies produced in Ireland.

BLACK BUSH

This is made at the Bushmills Distillery from triple distilled whiskies that have been aged for up to 18 years in oak barrels, most of which were previously used to hold sherry. Finally, the mature single malt (representing 80 per cent of the blend) is combined with single grain Irish whiskey, adding a touch of rich smoothness. It has a spicy nose with malty and nutty sweet sherry notes, and is rich and complex on the palate, as well as being rounded and slightly sweet, with a full finish.

BUSHMILLS

This is a malt whiskey aged for ten years and blended with a lighter grain whiskey. It is extremely soft, smooth and sweet with a slightly dry finish.

BUSHMILLS MALT

This is the only aged Irish single malt whiskey. Its water source is St Columb's Rill, which flows over a bed of basalt and adds its own character to the final whiskey. Aged for ten years in American oak barrels previously used to hold bourbon, the aroma is very clean with a balance between straight malt and subtle wood ageing. It has overtones of oloroso sherry, vanilla and honey on the nose, and a malty palate with some fruity sweetness redolent of apples and bananas, with a long, dry, soft oak and grainy finish.

CRESTED TEN

This is a full-bodied, rich whiskey that is matured for over ten years in oloroso sherry barrels, and blended with some younger grain whiskies. On the palate it has full-bodied sherry sweetness, toasted wood, fruit and spices with a warm, lingering finish.

JOHN JAMESON

This is the world's leading Irish whiskey, with the United Kingdom its largest export market. As a triple distilled whiskey made from barley and other cereals, it is aged in oak casks that were previously used to hold oloroso sherry or bourbon. This results in an exceptionally smooth, lemony nose with a sweet, biscuity palate, delicate woody, sweet character and a dry finish.

JAMESON 1780

1780 was the year in which John Jameson founded his distillery in Dublin, although this particular brand was launched in 1984. It is an exceptionally smooth whiskey, triple distilled and matured in oak casks for a minimum of 12 years, and it makes an ideal digestif.

KILBEGGAN

This is produced at the Kilbeggan Distillery, which was licensed in 1757. "Kilbeggan" means "little church" in Gaelic. The whiskey has an exceptionally smooth and rich flavour, reflecting its blend of aged grain and malt whiskies.

MIDLETON VERY RARE

This is a connoisseur's whiskey. It was launched in 1984 and is billed as the finest Irish whiskey. Malt whiskey is matured in bourbon casks for at least ten

years (typically 12 to 20 years), with only a small number being bottled each year, which explains why the year of production appears on the label. The velvety soft taste has hints of malt, toffee and nutmeg.

PADDY

This is a medium-bodied whiskey containing a blend of old malt whiskies, combined with pot still and grain whiskey that is matured in bourbon casks. It has a soft, sweet taste.

POWER'S GOLD LABEL

This is a full-flavoured blend of predominantly malt whiskey with some lighter grain whiskey. It has spicy, honeyed overtones that flourish on the palate.

THE TYRCONNELL SINGLE MALT

Originally distilled in 1762, this malt was subsequently named after the colt that won the 1876 Irish National Produce Stakes race with odds of 100 to 1. It has a fresh malty bouquet, and a smooth, subtly sweet flavour and a delicately dry finish.

AMERICAN WHISKEY

Since the introduction of whiskey to America by the original Irish and Scottish settlers, American whiskey has developed its own range of characteristics. Bourbon, the most renowned American whiskey, evolved during the late eighteenth century in Kentucky.

As the fame of Kentucky's more sophisticated style of whiskey spread to New Orleans, it came to be referred to as bourbon in order to distinguish it from other rye whiskies. It was named after Bourbon county in Kentucky where it was produced. The county had been named "Bourbon" in honour of the French royal family, who offered help during the war against Britain.

The sour mash principle was developed in Kentucky by the Scotsman Dr James Crow in 1835. It was a sensational innovation, and within a few years it had made Jim Crow's whiskey world-famous. Dr Crow was a physician and chemist and he developed his sour mash method by using the same strain of yeast in all batches of bourbon, which enhanced the flavour while also making it more consistent. A sour mash is prepared by starting

each fermentation process using yeast from the left-over mash of a previous fermentation. Making a sour mash whiskey takes longer, and the yield of whiskey is smaller (and consequently more expensive), but the subtlety of aromas and flavours results in a mellow and, above all, individual whiskey.

Bourbon's unique character is also partly due to the ageing process. A typical warehouse for ageing bourbon is a large rectangular structure with eight or more floors, with the sides and roof of the warehouse made of tin. Each storey is divided into three tiers of ricks, with each rick holding a row of barrels. Most distilleries build their warehouses on hilltops to expose them to seasonal changes.

Traditionally, distilleries rotated barrels during the maturation process so that each barrel spent a specified time at various temperatures and humidity levels in the warehouse, and in theory matured at the same rate. However, only some distilleries continue this practice, due to the

ABOVE: A typical scene in Kentucky.

LEFT: The Jim Beam Distillery.

GEORGE WASHINGTON

George Washington, the first president of the USA, initially distilled peach and apple brandy on his Mount Vernon plantation in Virginia, before also making rye whiskey. It became so popular that in 1798, the year after he left the presidency, Washington made more than $1,032 in profit from the enterprise – a significant sum at that time.

cost of labour and the cost of maintaining unused space (which is necessary to move the barrels).

Prior to bottling, bourbon is blended ("mingled" is the local term) to ensure consistency. For a standard brand, the mingling batch might be up to 200 barrels. However, for a more specialized "small batch" bourbon, the mingling batch may only be 20. The ultimate is a "single barrel" bourbon, which is, as the name suggests, taken from a single barrel. This style reflects the individual climate of the warehouse, and even the barrel's position within the warehouse.

ABOVE RIGHT: A magazine cartoon showing a scene from Prohibition (1919–33).

LEFT: A bottle of Early Times.

Several distilleries in Kentucky welcome visitors, including Heaven Hill, Wild Turkey, Ancient Age, Labrot & Graham, Four Roses and Cascade Distillery. The Oscar Getz Museum of Whiskey History is situated in Bardstown (the bourbon capital of the world), which also

hosts the annual Kentucky Bourbon Festival in September.

The Maker's Mark Distillery in Loretto, Kentucky, having been beautifully restored, is now a national historic landmark and the Quart House is believed to be America's oldest remaining "retail package store". It has been authentically restored to reflect the period long before Prohibition, when customers brought quart jugs to be filled from the store's whiskey casks.

The Jim Beam American Outpost in Clermont, Kentucky, takes visitors right through the bourbon-making process, including exhibitions of the ingredients, the distilling process, which includes America's oldest still, together with barrelling and ageing.

AMERICAN WHISKEY LIQUEURS

Referred to as "the grand old drink of the South", Southern Comfort is one of the most renowned American specialities, which originated in New Orleans during the 1860s. An enterprising young barkeeper named M.W. Heron developed a smooth, full-bodied spirit that he called Southern Comfort. Its popularity soon spread throughout the South, and it was in St Louis that Heron began to sell Southern Comfort in sealed bottles.

JACK DANIEL'S DISTILLERY

At the age of seven, Jack Daniel began his career when he went to work for Dan Call, a preacher who also made whiskey. Jack's natural interest in the whiskey-making process ensured that he was ready to take over the business at the youthful age of 13, when Dan Call offered to sell it to him.

As the fame of Jack Daniel's whiskey spread, he needed to find a site for a new distillery, which had to have a good source of water. He found his source on the outskirts of Lynchburg, a small farming community, where a large cave (known as Cave Spring) contains a deep limestone spring that supplies pure water all year round. The water is free of iron and other impurities that can ruin whiskey.

The distillery was established in what is known as Jack Daniel Hollow, with "hollow" being a local reference to a valley. When the American government began to regulate and tax whiskey distillers in the 1860s, the Jack Daniel Distillery was the first in America to be registered in 1866, when Jack was 17 years old. One of his descendants still runs Miss Mary Bobo's Boarding House in Lynchburg, dating from 1908, which can be visited.

ABOVE: The legendary Jack Daniel.

BELOW: Scenes from the distillery, showing casks being stored and two employees relaxing over a game of draughts (checkers).

AMERICAN WHISKEY DIRECTORY

The following guide explains the characteristics of selected whiskies produced in the USA.

JIM BEAM WHITE LABEL KENTUCKY BOURBON

Jacob Beam founded the Jim Beam Distillery in 1795, and his grandson James Beam joined the business in 1880. This bourbon has an elegant flowery aroma that includes hints of wood on the light, mellow lingering palate.

BLANTON'S KENTUCKY BOURBON

This single barrel bourbon does not carry an age state-ment because individual barrels reach peak maturity at different times. It has a rich flavour with a balanced sweetness.

BOOKER NOE'S KENTUCKY BOURBON

Booker Noe is the grandson of James Beam and the current master distiller at the Jim Beam Distillery. This is a distinguished eight-year-old limited edition bourbon.

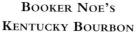

EARLY TIMES KENTUCKY BOURBON

This bourbon is produced at a distillery that was established in 1860. It is a deluxe whiskey with a smooth, distin-guished and mature flavour.

ELIJAH CRAIG 18 YEAR OLD SINGLE BARREL KENTUCKY BOURBON

A rarity being an 18-year-old single barrel style, the distinctive flavour of this bourbon is highly rewarding.

EVAN WILLIAMS KENTUCKY BOURBON

This is a sour mash, charcoal-filtered bourbon, which is produced at the Heaven Hill Distillery, established in 1783 in Bardstown, an area that has earned the appropriate nickname, Bourbonville, USA.

EVAN WILLIAMS SINGLE BARREL KENTUCKY BOURBON

The first vintage-dated single barrel bourbon, it has a perfectly balanced, smooth and mellow mature style, with complex flavours. The master distiller credits the use of traditional copper stills, the dis-tillery's own strain of natural yeast, and mat-uration in open rick warehouses, which are used in order to create its superior flavour.

FORESTER 1870 BOURBON

In 1870 this became the USA's first bottled bourbon (spirits were previously sold from barrels). It is highly aromatic, smooth and rich.

FOUR ROSES SINGLE BARREL RESERVE KENTUCKY BOURBON

The mash comprises around 60 per cent corn (maize), with the resulting spirit matured for eight years. Clearly there will be variations within this style, but it generally has spicy, floral notes, and a rich, mellow character reflecting the long maturation period.

FOUR ROSES YELLOW LABEL KENTUCKY BOURBON

This is aged for five years and blended using over ten different types of whiskey, which ultimately yield a fruity, nutty nose and a rich, soft, creamy flavour.

GENTLEMAN JACK RARE TENNESSEE WHISKEY

This is produced at one of the most famous distilleries in America, the Jack Daniel Distillery. It has a smooth yet distinctive rich flavour that reflects a certain degree of charcoal filtration.

GEORGE DICKEL & CO. ORIGINAL TENNESSEE WHISKEY

Rye, corn and barley are used in the mash, while charcoal "mellowing" means the whiskey is chilled before being fed through mellowing vats packed with charcoal. Additionally, a virgin wool blanket is placed on the top and bottom of the charcoal, as the longer and slower the filtration process,

the finer the end result. This yields a smooth, dry, mellow whiskey that allows traces of smoke, vanilla and white chocolate "woodiness" to emerge.

HENRY MCKENNA KENTUCKY BOURBON

The recipe dates from 1855 when Henry McKenna arrived from Scotland and began distilling whiskey in Kentucky. It is an ideal "sipping" whiskey and is produced at the renowned Heaven Hill Distilleries.

HENRY MCKENNA SINGLE BARREL KENTUCKY BOURBON

This is a ten-year-old super premium style, created by the master distiller at Heaven Hill.

JACK DANIEL'S TENNESSEE WHISKEY

Using corn and rye, this whiskey is charcoal-mellowed after distillation which yields a smooth, distinctive flavour. Produced in Lynchburg, Tennessee, the distillery was established in 1866. Jack Daniel's motto was, "every day we make it, we make it the best we can". True to his words, it is now one of the most famous whiskies in the world.

MAKER'S MARK KENTUCKY BOURBON

The mash includes winter wheat rather than rye, together with corn and barley malt, yielding a delicate and balanced, smooth whiskey, with a light spiciness, a hint of butterscotch and a deliberately short finish. Considered one of the finest bourbons, it was created in 1953. The distiller's philosophy was "rather than make a lot and pick out the best, make a little and have it all come out right", which certainly is true to the product.

REBEL YELL STRAIGHT KENTUCKY BOURBON

Named after the battle cry of the Southern Confederate Army in the

American Civil War, this was frequently referred to as "the spirit of the South". The recipe uses soft mature wheat and corn rather than rye, with the whiskey aged for four years in newly charred white oak barrels. It has a smooth, mellow character with a rich flavour.

SEAGRAM'S 7 CROWN BLENDED WHISKEY

This is an amalgamation of over 50 whiskies distilled from wheat, corn and rye, which are aged in charred oak barrels to produce a rich, deep, smooth flavour. This is an ideal base for mixed drinks and cocktails.

WILD TURKEY

The Ripy family first began distilling in 1885 in what is known as Wild Turkey Hill in Lawrenceburg, Kentucky. The brand, however, takes its name from the time when it was specially selected as the bourbon to be served at an annual wild turkey hunt in North Carolina. The sweetish, caramel nose, and full, smooth taste has hints of corn and vanilla with a luxuriant finish.

CANADIAN WHISKY

The earliest distillery in Canada is thought to have been established in 1668 by a Frenchman, Jean Talon, although the first recorded distillery was in Quebec City in 1769. By the 1840s there were over 200 distilleries in Upper and Lower Canada (Quebec), and the international reputation of Canadian whiskies was beginning to develop.

During the nineteenth century Canada had inexpensive land plus an abundant supply of grain, which were perfect conditions for the growth of the whisky industry. The rise of Canadian whisky was perpetuated by the emergence of two of the world's leading whisky distillers, Seagram and Hiram Walker Allied

Vintners, both of which originated in Canada.

In the mid-1850s, the eponymous Hiram Walker, an enterprising American and former apprentice in grocery stores, store owner and then grain merchant, purchased 468 acres of land just across the American border in Ontario, Canada. On this land he built a flour mill as well as a distillery.

By 1858 Hira Walker was selling flour, feed and whisky, which proved to be the origins of Canadian Club, one of the most renowned Canadian whiskies. Business prospered and the area surrounding the distillery grew into a small town named Walkerville. Whisky was sold to local grocers packaged in

ABOVE: The dramatic peaks of the Canadian Rockies.

LEFT: A painting of Hiram Walker, founder of the company bearing his name.

RIGHT: The Canadian Club Distillery, owned by Hiram Walker.

small barrels, branded with the company name and trademark. This practice became more refined when whisky was sold in large earthenware jugs.

When Hiram Walker progressed to bottling and sealing his whisky, in order to protect the quality, a brand name needed to be found. As Hiram Walker's whisky had long been enjoyed by members of gentlemen's clubs, the name "Club" seemed appropriate. By 1880 Hiram Walker had sales staff introducing Club whisky to a broader Canadian, as well as European, market. The success of this campaign led to the introduction of the brand to the USA in 1882, where it soon found favour.

However, not all Americans welcomed the success of this "foreign" brand, and some American distillers petitioned Washington for a bill that required Hiram Walker to label his whisky as "Canadian", in case consumers thought they were buying American whiskey. This law was passed in 1890, and it signalled the arrival of Canadian Club.

The Seagram empire is now a dominant force in the world of whisky. It dates from 1883 when Joseph Seagram

acquired the Waterloo Distillery in America. The company was subsequently acquired by Samuel Bronfman who founded Distillers Corporation – Seagram Ltd – in 1928, five years before the repeal of Prohibition in America. Convinced that liquor sales would eventually be legal there again, Bronfman took the financial risk of stockpiling and maturing whisky in Canada. When Prohibition was repealed in 1933, Bronfman controlled the world's largest stock of aged, top-quality whisky. Seagram's portfolio now also features single malt and blended Scotch whisky, American whiskey and numerous "local" whiskies from countries such as South Korea and even Brazil.

ABOVE AND LEFT: The Hiram Walker and the Seagram corporate logos.

ABOVE RIGHT: Samuel Bronfman, founder of Seagram.

RIGHT: Workers at one of the Seagram-owned distilleries check the casks.

CANADIAN WHISKY DIRECTORY

The following guide explains the characteristics of selected popular whiskies produced in Canada.

CANADIAN CLUB

Canadian Club whiskies are produced from a combination of rye, corn (maize), barley malt and rye malt. They have an uncommon lightness of taste, texture and colour. Styles include Canadian Club Classic 12 year old, a

super premium whisky with a rich, aromatic taste presented in a decanter style bottle. Canadian Club 20 year old has depth and complexity, and is presented in an elegant gift tin.

CANADIAN MIST

This whisky uses only top-quality grains harvested from the fields of Ontario and pure water from the Georgian Bay, which is one of the world's cleanest and freshest water sources located approximately 120 kilometres (75 miles) northwest of Toronto. This three-year-

old whisky has a distinguished bouquet and mellow character, reflecting the use of charred oak barrels for maturation.

CROWN ROYAL

This was specially blended from corn and rye whiskies to commemorate a grand tour of Canada made by King George VI and Queen Elizabeth of Great Britain. The smooth, rich and elegant style reflects its regal origins.

GIBSON'S FINEST 12 YEAR OLD
Aged in white oak casks, this has a rich aroma and smooth, full-bodied flavour.

HARWOOD CANADIAN
This is fully-flavoured, yet with the archetypal mild and smooth character.

SCHENLEY GOLDEN WEDDING
This renowned blend was introduced in 1856. It is a full-bodied whisky, which is very smooth on the palate.

SCHENLEY ORIGINAL FINE CANADIAN
Introduced in 1955, this highly traditional rye whisky has repeatedly won numerous prestigious awards. This is a blend of various selected eight-year-old whiskies that are aged in white oak casks, and it has a wonderful balance that is particularly mellow and smooth in character.

SEAGRAM'S VO
Matured for six years, this has a light, smooth, mellow body.

WISER'S SPECIAL BLEND
This balanced nose features spices such as vanilla, together with fresh wood, while a smooth, mild oak palate entails subtle sweetness and a compact finish. The deluxe ten-year-old has a rich nose with dried fruits and oak that lead to a rounded, full-bodied palate with rich toffee and toasted grains.

WHISKY AROUND THE WORLD

Many "local" whiskies are produced around the world, in countries such as Japan, South Korea, Wales and Spain. While they may not have the international cachet of Scotch, Irish, American and Canadian whiskies, these "local" brands nevertheless have an individual style and a loyal following.

JAPAN

The Japanese love of luxury goods has helped to place whisky on a pedestal, and while Japan is a vital export market for numerous Scotch and American distillers, home-produced whisky also has an established heritage.

Japanese whisky dates from 1923 when Shinjiro Torii, the founder of Suntory, now a multinational company with

diversified interests, built Japan's first distillery in the Yamazaki Valley outside Kyoto. It was an area that offered the most favourable conditions for whisky production. As an accomplished blender with a highly developed olfactory sense, Shinjiro Torii launched Japan's first whisky, Suntory Shirofuda (still marketed as Suntory White), in 1929. Further launches that significantly raised the cachet of Japanese whisky included Kakubin in 1937 as well as Old in 1940.

ABOVE: Casks stored at one of the Suntory distilleries in Japan.

LEFT: A view of Suntory, a company that is one of the most successful producers of Japanese whiskies.

malt whisky, Hibiki and Crest 12 year old, which were launched in 1989 as part of the company's 90th anniversary celebrations, and Royal, Reserve, Old, Kakubin and Shirokaku blended whiskies. The Suntory Museum of Whisky details the history, culture and technology of whisky production in Japan. Suntory, which was founded in 1899, subsequently became established as an international conglomerate, with food and pharmaceutical operations in addition to producing whisky.

SOUTH KOREA

The large multinational drinks company, Seagram, whose comprehensive whisky portfolio includes among others, The Glenlivet, Chivas Regal, Four Roses and Crown Royal, has also initiated "local" whisky production in various countries. In South Korea, a joint venture produces Gold Classic and Secret, which are both renowned brands.

Suntory also operates two other distilleries in Japan. The Hakushu Distillery, built in 1973 amidst a scenic forest, features a cellar and various types of copper pot stills which produce a range of malt whiskies. The nearby Hakushu Higashi Distillery was established in 1981, and in fact shares the same water source as the Hakushu Distillery.

While Suntory has diversified and also produces a range of brandies, gins, vodkas, rums, tequilas and liqueurs, whisky remains the core spirit. The range includes Yamazaki pure

LEFT TO RIGHT: A selection of some of Suntory's brands of whisky, including Suntory Royal, Yamazaki pure malt whisky and Hibiki.

SPAIN

Spain's only whisky distillery is Destilerias Y Crianza del Whisky (DYC) in Segovia, which malts, distils, blends and matures whisky on the premises using raw materials sourced in Spain. Two styles are produced, DYC 5 year old and DYC 8 year old, which are a blend of malt and grain whisky. Whisky DYC is only sold in Spain, where its success is such that it accounts for 25 per cent of the whisky market. It is usually drunk neat or mixed with cola or water.

Established in 1959, DYC's first whiskies were available four years later, having been matured in oak barrels. Production commenced after strict new regulations for making whisky were introduced by the Spanish government. These regulations had stipulated improved production facilities, raw materials and production processes (which also resulted in a certain number of Spanish distilleries closing down). In 1992 DYC was acquired by the sherry producer Domecq, which subsequently merged with the multinational conglomerate Allied Lyons, and DYC is now part of the Allied Domecq Group.

WALES

Welsh whisky evolved from the historic "bragget" or "seet ale", a type of beer originally brewed from barley by monks on Bardsey, a small island off the Welsh coast. When the knowledge of distillation reached Wales, this brew was distilled to make a spirit that was referred to as "Chwisgi" by the Welsh Celts, and it was made more palatable by adding honey and herbs. It was initially used as a medicinal drink, but was also considered to be a great aphrodisiac.

After the dissolution of the monasteries, distilling was principally undertaken by farmers as a way of using up their surplus grain. It was in the early eighteenth century that the first commercial distillery was founded in Pembrokeshire by the Evan Williams family of Dale. Another distillery was

LEFT: *A bottle of DYC whisky, produced in Spain.*

ABOVE: *Swn y Mor is a prominent Welsh whisky, produced at the Brecon Brewery.*

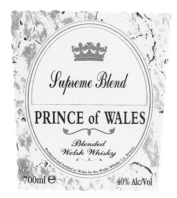

established in 1888 by Robert Willis and a Mr Price of Rhiwlas, with the company having an issued share capital of £100,000, which was then quite a substantial figure. However, in 1906 the company then closed down in the face of a powerful temperance movement which swept Wales.

It was not until 1974 that Welsh whisky appeared again. Using a small cellar in Brecon, in the south of Wales, Dafydd Gittins began blending Swn y Don Welsh "Chwisgi". In 1975 the enterprise moved to small premises behind the Camden Arms Inn, in Brecon. It was here that the Brecon Brewery was formed and the evolution of Swn y Mor Welsh Whisky began. It took six more years to perfect the recipe, which was as close as possible to the original Welsh whiskies.

ABOVE: A bottle and labels for the Prince of Wales, a popular Welsh whisky.

RIGHT: The Brecon Beacons, Wales, home of the Brecon Brewery.

In 1982 the company moved to its present location at Brecon's Parc Menter in the heart of the beautiful Brecon Beacons. In addition to Swn y Mor blended whisky, three styles of Prince of Wales whisky are produced, all aged in oak casks. Prince of Wales Supreme Blend and Prince of Wales 12 year old have an impressive bouquet that leads on to a rich, mellow flavour, while Prince of Wales Special Reserve has a distinguished bouquet and smooth malt flavour. The company also produces a range of other spirits and liqueurs.

COCKTAILS

Cocktails immediately create a sense of occasion and several famous cocktails have been created in honour of whisky. Some recipes are ideally prepared with a cocktail shaker, which mixes the ingredients and ensures they are thoroughly chilled by ice. Alternatively, stir the mixture in a large jug. All the following cocktails serve one person.

MINT JULEP
This well-established cocktail originated in the southern states of America. Add fresh mint leaves according to taste.

INGREDIENTS
15ml/1 tbsp caster sugar
8–10 fresh mint leaves
15ml/1 tbsp hot water
2 measures/45ml/3 tbsp bourbon or whisky

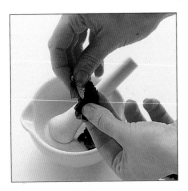

1 Place the sugar in a pestle and mortar or bowl. Tear the mint leaves into small pieces and add them to the sugar.

2 Bruise the mint leaves with the pestle (or a spoon if using a bowl), to release their flavour and to combine with the sugar.

3 Add the hot water to the mint leaves and grind everything together well.

4 Spoon the mixture into a snifter glass or brandy balloon and half fill it with some crushed ice.

5 Add the bourbon or whisky to the snifter glass.

6 Stir until the outside of the glass has frosted. Allow to stand for 1–2 minutes, to let the ice melt slightly and to dilute the drink a little.

MANHATTAN

You can also use sweet vermouth, dry vermouth or both (add a dash of angostura bitters if using just one).

INGREDIENTS

2 measures/45ml/3 tbsp rye whiskey
1/4 measure/5ml/1 tsp dry French vermouth
1/4 measure/5ml/1 tsp sweet Italian vermouth
lemon rind and a maraschino cherry, to decorate

1 Pour the whiskey and both vermouths into a bar glass filled with ice. Stir well for 30 seconds to mix and then leave to chill.

3 Pare away a small strip of lemon rind with a canelle knife. Tie a knot, to release its oil, and add to the cocktail.

2 Strain the mixture, on the rocks or straight up, into a chilled cocktail glass.

4 To decorate, add a maraschino cherry with its stalk left intact.

VARIATION

Create a Skyscraper by adding the following ingredients to the Manhattan recipe: a dash of angostura bitters and a teaspoon of maraschino cherry juice, then top up with some ginger ale to taste.

GALL BRACER

Serve this drink on the rocks, in a tumbler for a man or in a delicate long-stemmed cocktail glass for a woman.

INGREDIENTS
2 dashes angostura bitters
2 dashes grenadine
2 measures/45ml/3 tbsp whisky
strip of lemon rind
maraschino cherry, to decorate (optional)

1 Half-fill a bar glass with ice. Add the angostura bitters, grenadine and whisky and stir well.

3 Hold the lemon rind and squeeze out the oil and juices into the cocktail. Discard.

2 Place some ice in a short tumbler and pour the cocktail over it through a strainer.

4 Add a maraschino cherry, for decoration, if you like and serve immediately.

VARIATION

To make a Gall Bracer into a longer drink, top it up with either soda or sparkling mineral water. Alternatively, for a cocktail called a Gall Trembler substitute gin for the whisky and add extra dashes of bitters to taste.

SEA DOG

This long whisky drink with a citrus twist can be made sweeter by adding the second sugar lump.

INGREDIENTS
1–2 sugar cubes
2 dashes angostura bitters
2 orange and 2 lemon wedges
2/3 measure/15ml/1 tbsp whisky
1 measure/22.5ml/1¹/2 tbsp Benedictine
2 measures/45ml/2fl oz/3 tbsp soda water, chilled
maraschino cherry, to decorate

1 *Put the sugar cube into a Collins glass. Add the bitters so they soak into the sugar.*

3 *When some of the citrus juices are released add plenty of cracked ice.*

2 *Add the orange and lemon wedges and press the juices from the fruit with a muddler.*

4 *Add the whisky and the Benedictine to the mixture.*

5 *Mix the ingredients together well with a swizzle stick for about 20 seconds and top up the glass with the chilled soda water.*

6 *Serve with the muddler so that more juice can be pressed. Decorate with a maraschino cherry that has its stalk left intact and serve.*

OLD-FASHIONED

Grind up a sugar lump. Mix with a little angostura bitters and give the mixture a good shake. Pour into a tumbler with plenty of ice and a generous measure of Canadian or straight rye whiskey. Throw in a twist of lemon peel, a slice of orange and a maraschino cherry to decorate, and serve with a swizzle stick. *LEFT*

SARACEN

Shake a measure of Scotch whisky, half a measure each of Glayva and dry sherry and a dash of orange bitters with ice. Pour into a tumbler and add a splash of soda. Decorate with a piece of orange rind. *BELOW LEFT*

BUNNY HUG

Shake equal measures of gin, Scotch whisky and pastis and pour into a cocktail glass. *BELOW RIGHT*

WHISKY MAC

This drink is very popular. Mix half-and-half Scotch whisky with green ginger wine, and serve it without ice. *RIGHT*

RUSTY NAIL

Serve equal measures of Drambuie and Scotch whisky, over ice if you like.

BOSTON

Shake equal measures of dry Madeira and bourbon with 2.5ml/½ tsp caster sugar. Add an egg yolk and strain into a glass. Sprinkle with grated nutmeg and serve. *BELOW LEFT*

WHISKY SOUR

Shake 2 measures/45ml/3 tbsp whisky, 25ml/1½ tbsp each lemon and lime juices, 15ml/1 tbsp sugar syrup and 5ml/1 tsp caster sugar. Strain over ice cubes into a glass and decorate with lemon wedges. *BELOW RIGHT*

INDEX

ACKNOWLEDGEMENTS

The following pictures are reproduced with the kind permission of: The Advertising Archives: 15tl, *Highland Games*; 15br, *King George IV*. Real Ireland Design Limited: 40–1, *Irish Pubs* by Liam Blake. The Bridgeman Art Library: 2, *Loch Katrine* by George F. Robson; 7, *Rob Roy and the Baillie* by John W. Nicol, courtesy of Sheffield City Art Galleries; 8t, *The Irish Whiskey Still* by Sir David Wilkie, courtesy of the National Gallery of Scotland; 11br, *The Smugglers* by George Morland, courtesy of Fitzwilliam Museum, University of Cambridge. e.t. archive: 8br, *Dr Johnson* by Sir Joshua Reynolds, Courage Breweries; 9l, *Clans of the Scottish Highlands – Buchanan* by R.R. McIan; 15c, *Johnnie Walker Whisky, 1929*; 45tl, *George Washington*, Musée Versailles. The Kobal Collection: 12t, *The Roaring Twenties*, courtesy of Warner Bros/First National. The Still Moving Picture Co: 19bl, *The River Spey* by Angus Johnston; 19br, *Barley Field* by Alasdair MacFarlane; 25bl, *Piper, Glen Garry* by Marius Alexander; 20b, *Alt-a-Bhain Distillery*, 22tl, *Whisky Nosing*, 24t, *Suilven* and 25r, *Robert Burns, Alloway* all by Doug Corrance. The Visual Arts Library: 3, *Belle Jardinière*, courtesy of Collection Kharbine-Tapabor; 15tr, *Thanksgiving 1942*, 15bl, *Haig Whisky* and 45tr, *Le Petit Journal*, all courtesy of Selva. Jaya Wardene Photo Library: 50t, *Canadian Rockies*.

The publishers would like to thank the following people and organizations for their contributions to this book and/or for supplying additional pictures: Robert Scott at Milroy's of Soho Ltd: Alfred Dunhill Scotch Whisky Ltd: 14br. Allied Distillers Ltd: 34l. Allied Domecq Group: 56l. Blanton's Distilling Co: 14bl. Debbie Brooks at Brown-Forman Beverages Worldwide: 23t, 45bl, 47r, 52r. Campbell Distillers Ltd: 28bl, 30bl, 42t+r, 43t. CSPR: 18t. Cutty Sark Scots Whisky: 35bl.

Douglas Laing & Co: 14tr. Matthew Gloag & Son Ltd: 21bl+r. Hagley Museum and Library: 51bl+br+tr. Heaven Hill Distilleries: 23bl, 48br. Highland Park Distillery: 10bl. Hiram Walker & Sons Ltd: 50bl+r, 51tl. Invergordon Distillers: 9r. Irish Distillers Ltd: 8l, 13tr, 38t+bl, 39tl (courtesy of Robert and Maria Waters of Tigin Irish Pub, USA), 39tc, 39tr, 39br, 42bl, 43t and back cover. Jack Daniel's Distillery: 5, 12r, 44t, 46 and back cover. Jim Beam Distillery: 44b. J&B: 16t, 21t, 32bl, 33t. Joseph E. Seagram & Sons Ltd: 26bl, 27l+tr, 31bl, 32t, 34t, 36t. The Kentucky Distillers Association: 13tl, 18tr, 22tr. Suntory Limited: 23br, 54, 55tr+b. Lucy Penrose at United Distillers: 4, 10tl+tr, 15bc, 19t, 22b, 24bl, 25t, 26t, 27tl, 48t, 49t, 53bl+t. Wales Tourist Board Photo Library: 57br. William Grants & Sons, Inc: 14tl, 20t, 24br, 30br and back cover.

l=left, r=right, t=top, b=bottom, c=centre

The author would like to thank the following organizations:
The Scotch Whisky Association, United Distillers, Mulcaster & Associates, Seagram, Allied Domecq, International Distillers & Vintners, Matthew Gloag, William Grant, Campbell Distillers, Irish Distillers, Kentucky Distillers' Association, Heaven Hill Distilleries, Jim Beam, Maker's Mark Distillery, United Distillers Canada, Association of Canadian Distillers, Suntory.

USEFUL ADDRESSES

The Scotch Whisky Association
20 Atholl Crescent
Edinburgh EH3 8HF
Scotland
United Kingdom

The Irish Whiskey Visitor Centre
Irish Distillers Ltd
Bow Street
Dublin 7
Ireland

Kentucky Distillers' Association
110 West Main
Springfield
Kentucky 40069
USA

Association of Canadian Distillers
90 Rue Sparks Street
Suite 1100
Ottawa, Ontario
Canada